SUMMER SHADOWS ON CHESTNUT STREET

HISTORIC SALEM

IN FOUR SEASONS

THE CUSTOM HOUSE (1819)

A CAMERA IMPRESSION BY
SAMUEL CHAMBERLAIN

HASTINGS HOUSE · PUBLISHERS · NEW YORK

STANLEY F. BAR   Publish

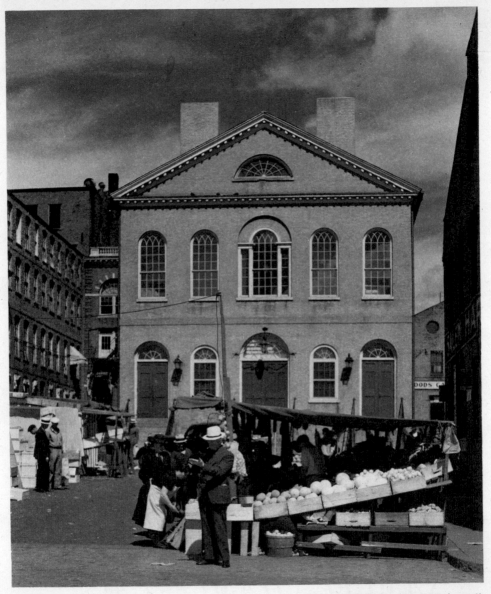

THE MARKET HOUSE (1816)

THE CITY ALMSHOUSE (1816), CHARLES BULFINCH, ARCHITECT

FOREWORD

NO five foot bookshelf could hold the volumes which have been written about Salem. So many of them have done justice to their illustrious subject that a new book may seem almost presumptuous without a word of explanation. It is hoped that this pictorial volume on Salem will be justified for two reasons. First, it is a contemporary record of historic Salem. Time passes quickly, even in Salem, and it causes startling and sometimes irreparable changes. The dated document has a certain value, be it an old engraving, a panoramic painting, a bird's-eye sketch by a schoolboy or an old photograph. Secondly, though Salem has been treated handsomely by the printed word, good photographic records of it are rare indeed. Yet it is an American landmark of extra-ordinary significance, and frequently, great beauty. The observant visitor to Salem carries away a vivid mental picture which can be preserved, or at least refreshed, by good pictures. If this small book can serve this one purpose, without any pretense of being a guide or a history, it will be privileged indeed.

One has to wander a good deal, and skip a lot, to see the best of old Salem. These pages do just that. They attempt to group most of the historic landmarks together, omitting the rest, and a certain amount of wandering results. Along Salem's three most significant streets, Essex, Federal and Chestnut, they fall into a fairly orderly stroll, however. Some of Salem's most beautiful moments are in winter, when few visitors see it. To present a more revealing picture of the city's many moods, these photographs have been taken in all seasons of the year.

The Salem of Roger Conant and Governor Bradstreet, of the tragic witchcraft delusion, of clipper ships and merchant princes, the Salem of Nathaniel Haw-thorne demands the eloquence of the written word to do it justice. But the real-istic Salem of today, still rich with dramatic reminders of the past, is a subject to which the camera may aspire. If a little of Salem's beauty has been caught by this roving lens, its ambition is fulfilled.

CHARTER STREET

The Pioneers' Village

Salem was like this three centuries ago, when the ship "Arbella" brought Governor John Winthrop and the Company to the tiny settlement in the wilderness. Founded by Roger Conant in 1626, and then known as Naumkeag, it consisted of a handful of rude habitations bordering a secluded cove, and dominated by the steep-roofed "Governor's Faire House." A vivid picture of the pioneer life of those epic days of 1630 has been preserved in the "Pioneers' Village," a reconstruction made in commemoration 300 years later. Here the primitive huts, dugouts and wigwams of Naumkeag are faithfully reproduced. A replica of the "Arbella" is at the water's edge. The same flowers and herbs which flourished then still grow in the gardens.

DUGOUTS AND BARK-COVERED WIGWAMS WERE THE FIRST PRIMITIVE SHELTERS IN SALEM, FOLLOWED BY CRUDE THATCHED CABINS *(below)*

THE PIONEERS' VILLAGE

Graphic reminders of the hardships and the ingenuity of the early pioneers are found in this reconstructed community. Here are the brick kilns and the saw-pits *(opposite top)* such as were used by the first builders. At the crossroads are the stocks and pillory for unlucky miscreants *(opposite bottom)*. In front of Arbella House is the soap cauldron, suspended from a crude tripod, where grease and lye were boiled *(right)*. In the salt works *(below)* sea water was evaporated in shallow pans to obtain salt, a process which was hastened by a wood fire burning underneath.

THE SALT WORKS *(below)*   **ARBELLA HOUSE**

GALLOWS HILL

The delusion of witchcraft which had afflicted the Old World during the 17th century descended upon Salem Village (now Danvers) in 1692 with terrifying results. Spreading from the mischievous antics of young girls, whose imaginations were fired by the voodoo tales of a West Indian slave woman, the plague of witchcraft flared up in many parts of Salem, causing more than a score of victims before it subsided. Nineteen innocent people were hanged from trees on this hill during that dreadful summer.

The "Witch House," so called because it was the home of Jonathan Corwin, one of the judges of the witchcraft court, is still standing much as it was in 1692, save for the inglorious appendage of a Victorian drug-store.

A noteworthy and little-changed survivor of those troubled days is the Narbonne House (built before 1671) at 71 Essex Street. The small door on the left led to a "cent" shop which was squeezed under the steep lean-to roof.

THE PICKERING HOUSE

Flamboyant wooden Gothic externals, added to this house in 1841, disguise its true antiquity, for it is probably the oldest dwelling now standing in Salem proper, dating from 1660. A cast iron fireback of this date was found in the house, the work of Elisha Jenks of Saugus, the first iron founder in the Colonies. The house stands on a piece of land granted to John Pickering in 1637 and is still occupied by his lineal descendants. Colonel Timothy Pickering, soldier, statesman and member of George Washington's Cabinet, was born here in 1745. The house is located at 18 Broad Street.

The House of Seven Gables

Rare is the schoolboy who is not familiar with the romance laid in this weather-beaten old house, which is perhaps the reason that it is the most celebrated, most visited spot in Salem. Built in 1668 and later restored, the house was the home of Susan Ingersoll, the spinster cousin of Nathaniel Hawthorne, at the time when the novelist was at work on his famous romance. The house was restored in 1910 and is now open to the public. Located on the water's edge, it is a spot of unforgettable charm and tranquillity.

THE HOUSE OF SEVEN GABLES—IN WINTER AND IN SUMMER

The miniature shop of the House of Seven Gables is said to have served as the toll-house for the old Marblehead ferry in the 18th century. Now it is filled with a beguiling display of old-fashioned toys, figurines, candies, prints, ship models and cards.

The grounds of the House of Seven Gables are enriched by two other ancient structures, the Hathaway House *(opposite)*, built in 1682, and the Retire Becket House *(page 17)*, the core of which dates back to 1655. These were rescued from an uncertain fate and moved here to form a thoroughly Elizabethan group, clustered about an old-fashioned flower garden.

THE HATHAWAY HOUSE, "THE OLD BAKERY," (1682), IN CONTRASTING SEASONS

A CORNER IN THE KITCHEN-LIVING ROOM OF THE HATHAWAY HOUSE

The Hathaway House was formerly known as "The Old Bakery" before it was moved from its site on Washington Street in 1911. Most of its superb carved timbers have been preserved. The Retire Becket House *(opposite)* was for six generations the home of the Beckets, a family of famous ship designers.

The House of Seven Gables group was restored and assembled through the generosity of Miss Caroline O. Emmerton. It is also a center of neighborhood settlement work, and all profits are devoted to this worthy philanthropy.

A WINTRY IMPRESSION OF THE RETIRE BECKET HOUSE

DERBY WHARF

During the great days of Salem shipping in the early 19th century, this narrow inlet was lined with sailing vessels from every corner of the globe. Now undredged and unkempt, it was once the scene of the greatest shipping activity in America. Fortunes were made by the intrepid young sea captains who docked here after long voyages to the Orient, unloading strange cargoes of spices, silks and ivory, fans, feathers and chinaware, coffee, tea and gum-copal. Derby Wharf will soon regain much of its former glory, for its restoration has been undertaken by the Government. At the head of the inlet can be seen the ivy-covered Crowninshield House and the strategically located Custom House.

THE RICHARD DERBY HOUSE (1762)

Located at the head of the wharf which bears its name, this Georgian mansion is the oldest brick house now standing in Salem (168 Derby Street). It was built by Richard Derby, the first of a succession of merchant princes by that name. Two chimneys and four fireplaces are built into each of its brick ends. Besides its classic doorway and superb stair rail, the house is noteworthy for its fine panelling which, in some rooms is painted a subtle olive green, in others a maroon or a powder blue. The house forms a part of the Government restoration.

9

Of the two structures at the head of Derby Wharf, the imposing brick residence built by Benjamin W. Crowninshield *(left)* is the oldest. It was erected in 1810 from designs by Samuel McIntyre. Crowninshield was Secretary of the Navy under Presidents Madison and Monroe, and the latter was once a guest in this house during a four day visit to Salem in 1817. It now serves as a home for aged women (180 Derby Street).

On the right is the Custom House, built in 1819 in the best Federal tradition. The portico *(opposite)* is one of the most delicate bits of architectural detail in Salem. Nathaniel Hawthorne was named surveyor of customs in 1846, and spent three years in an office in this building. In his leisure moments at the Custom House the novelist evolved the plot for "The Scarlet Letter."

THE CUSTOM HOUSE AFTER A SUMMER SHOWER

22

Nathaniel Hawthorne

The name of the great American novelist is always closely associated with Salem. It was his birthplace, the scene of his lonely boyhood and his subsequent struggles to work at occupations ill suited to his sensitive nature. It was Salem, enlivened and enriched by his vivid imagination, which Hawthorne used as a setting for many of his writings. In recognition of Salem's greatest literary figure is this monument, the work of Bela Pratt.

In the northwest chamber of the old gambrel roofed house shown below, Hawthorne was born, July 4, 1804.

HAWTHORNE'S BIRTHPLACE *(below)*, 27 UNION STREET

PORCH FROM THE
GRIMSHAWE HOUSE

GRIMSHAWE HOUSE

The scene of one of the happy chapters of Hawthorne's life and, strangely
enough, of some of the more grisly episodes of his books, was the Grimshawe
House, at 53 Charter Street. It was the home of Sophia Amelia Peabody, Hawthorne's childhood playmate and later his wife, at the time of their courtship. The
house and its handsome doorway are accurately described in "Dr. Grimshawe's
Secret." The original doorway is now preserved in the outdoor museum of the
Essex Institute.

Hawthorne's familiarity with the interior of the Turner-Ingersoll House *(opposite)*, later known as the "House of Seven Gables," is well known. Another
house closely connected with his name is at 14 Mall Street. It was in this house
that he wrote "The Scarlet Letter" while beset by personal worries.

THE LIVING ROOM IN THE "HOUSE OF SEVEN GABLES"; *(below)* THE GREAT
CHAMBER OR "PHOEBE'S ROOM"

HERE
LYETH BURIED
BODY OF CAPT
RICHARD MORE
AGED 84 YEARS
DIED 1692
A MAYFLOWER
PILGRIM

Hawthorne often wandered through the "Burying Point," adjoining the Grimshawe House, and in his writings often used this venerable graveyard, which dates from 1637. In it are buried Governor Bradstreet, Chief Justice Lynde, Samuel McIntyre and Reverend John Higginson. It also contains the unique gravestone of Richard More, who came over on the "Mayflower" as a boy. It is the only known original tombstone of a Mayflower passenger.

TOMBSTONE OF RICHARD MORE   2

The Essex Institute

Flanked by the feudal towers of the Armory on one side and by the suave facade of the Pingree House on the other, the Essex Institute and its museum occupy a significant place in the culture of New England. Its museum stands on the site of the original house of Governor Bradstreet. Devoted principally to the art, history and genealogy of Salem and its environs, the Essex Institute possesses a superb library on these subjects, including the "Ward China Library" which is probably without equal in this country. The museum contains a collection of some 300 historic paintings and an infinite and fascinating exhibit of relics from the early days of Salem. Several of Salem's most noteworthy houses have come under the Institute's protective care.

2

THE PINGREE HOUSE (1804), Samuel McIntyre, Architect

A prized possession of the Essex Institute is the Gardner-White-Pingree House, the finest house in brick built by Samuel McIntyre. The refinement of its doorway *(opposite)* and its subtle proportions reveal the great carver-architect at his peak. Born in Salem in 1757, the son of a joiner who taught him the carpenter's trade, this astonishing craftsman devoted practically all of his talent to the town of his birth, and died here in 1811. Without doubt the most accomplished woodcarver in America in his time, he was a gifted architect as well. His influence upon the beauty of Salem, and upon Federal architecture, was incalculable. Two of his masterpieces, the South Church and the celebrated Derby mansion, have disappeared, but many noble structures remain as reminders of his skill and his ceaseless industry.

Contrasting Interiors

In the outdoor museum of the Essex Institute is the observation cupola rescued from the Pickman-Derby-Brookhouse mansion (1764), which once overlooked Salem Harbor. A hole was left in one of the window panes for the watchful shipowner's telescope.

THE JOHN WARD HOUSE (1684) IS ALMOST MEDIAEVAL IN CHARACTER (ESSEX INSTITUTE)

The atmospheric East India Marine Hall, built in 1824 and dedicated by President John Quincy Adams, now houses the Peabody Museum, a matchless assemblage of marine objects, paintings and ship models, and the Hall of Natural History.

SHIPS IN SALEM—AS THEY *WERE*
A reproduction of the ship "Arbella," which brought Governor Winthrop
with the charter of the Massachusetts Bay Company to Salem in June 1630.

SHIPS IN SALEM—AS THEY *ARE*—Yachts on Their Spring Overhauling

ST. PETER'S CHURCH

Salem has not been fortunate in keeping its old churches. One of the last tragedies was the loss of McIntyre's superb South Church on Chestnut Street, destroyed by fire in 1903. Among the survivors is the gaunt but picturesque St. Peter's Church, built in 1833. In its tower hangs a bell which has been ringing in Salem for almost two centuries. It was cast in England and first rang in 1740 from the tower of the first Episcopal Church, long since destroyed.

Washington Square

Bordering the broad wooded triangle of Washington Square, which is Salem's "Common," are imposing mansions from the prosperous marine period. None is more impressive than the Andrew-Safford House *(below)*, built in 1818. Its elaborate doorway, double balustrade and lofty side portico help to explain why it was once considered the most costly residence in New England. The stern bronze figure of Roger Conant, the city's founder, dominates one corner of the Square. It is the work of Henry H. Kitson.

HOUSES ON THE "COMMON"—(*above*) THE FORRESTER HOUSE, NOW THE BER-
TRAM HOME FOR AGED MEN. (*opposite*) THE SHIMMERING FENCE OF THE BALDWIN-LYMAN
HOUSE (1818).

HOUSE AT 52 ESSEX STREET

A variation in Federal mansions is the type with two brick ends, between which wooden frame construction is used. This old house, built about 1800, is a good example. In the foreground is a weathered corner of the Stephen Daniel House, a veteran of 1682.

The Hosmer-Townsend-Waters House *(opposite)* at No. 80 Washington Square is one of McIntyre's most original designs, built in 1795. It has two exquisite doorways and a huge central chimney running through the center of the house.

I

ESSEX STREET

Beyond the snow-covered fenceposts of the Ropes Mansion is the granite tower of First Church (1835).

314 ESSEX STREET

The Lindall-Gibbs-Osgood House (1773) where Benjamin Thompson, later Count Rumford, soldier and inventor, lived as a boy. Rumford ovens can still be found in Salem houses.

THE ROPES MEMORIAL—(1719)—318 ESSEX STREET
A wintry impression of this friendly mansion, which preserves the atmosphere of
a wealthy home of Salem's flourishing merchant days with remarkable accuracy.

4

THE FACADE OF THE ROPES MEMORIAL HAS A MARITIME FEELING

THE COACH HOUSE OF THE EMMERTON HOUSE REFLECTS THE
OPULENCE OF NINETEENTH CENTURY SALEM.

SALT AIR SEEMS CLOSE TO THIS SUNNY SEGMENT OF ESSEX STREET.

THE CLARK-MORGAN HOUSE—358 ESSEX STREET

In this house of many pediments the Morgan sisters kept a Dame school some fifty years ago.

The Cabot-Endicott-Low-Ives House *(opposite bottom)* at 365 Essex Street is one of the finest in New England, noted for its interior woodwork. Built in 1748 by Joseph Cabot, it was long the residence of Wm. Crowninshield Endicott, Secretary of War in Cleveland's cabinet. The English statesman, Joseph Chamberlain, and General Sherman were entertained here.

40 SUMMER STREET   *Salem Doorways*   RICHARD DERBY HOUSE

52 ESSEX STREET   146 FEDERAL STREET

74 WASHINGTON SQUARE
(MCINTYRE) 1805   *Salem Doorways*   116-118 FEDERAL STREET
380 ESSEX STREET (MCINTYRE) 1797   25 FLINT STREET

THE STEARNS HOUSE (Now East India House Inn) 384 ESSEX STREET

Built in 1776, this house has the distinction of possessing some of McIntyre's earliest work. He added this handsome Doric porch in 1785.

McINTYRE'S COOK-OLIVER HOUSE (1804) 142 FEDERAL STREET

Federal Street is Samuel McIntyre's true path of glory. Several of his masterpieces repose behind the shining white fences of this verdant street.

FEDERAL STREET, THE SETTING FOR McINTYRE'S MASTERPIECES

A detail of the Coo
Oliver House. The s
perb gate-posts, han
tooled by McInty
and much of the in
rior finish was rescu
from the ill-fated El
Hasket Derby Ma
sion. This house
one of the most n
table examples of t
carver-architect's
handicraft.

THE ASSEMBLY HALL (1782) 138 FEDERAL STREET—Samuel McIntyre, Architect

Built expressly for receptions, balls and banquets, this building shows McIntyre in a festive mood. The porch, bedecked with a grapevine frieze, and the iron fence are later.

3

A WINTRY IMPRESSION OF THE ASSEMBLY HALL

Lafayette was entertained here in 1784 at the time of his first triumphant tour, and Washington danced at a ball given here in his honor in 1789. Following those memorable days it became a private dwelling.

The house at 135 Federal Street (*opposite*) is another McIntyre house, built in 1804 and restored about 1860.

THE GEORGE M. WHIPPLE HOUSE (1804) 2 ANDOVER STREET

The Peirce-Nichols House (*opposite*) has been called, with little exaggeration, the finest wooden house in New England. Done in the first flush of McIntyre's artistic career, when he was twenty-five years old, it is the best example of his genius now standing. He worked for years on its interior woodwork, the last of which was completed in 1801. The mansion was built by Jerathmiel Peirce, a prosperous East Indian merchant whose ships, laden with goods from the Orient, docked at a nearby wharf. A great deal of atmosphere is lent by the stable and carriage buildings (*page 59*).

THE PEIRCE-NICHOLS HOUSE (1781) 80 FEDERAL STREET
SAMUEL MCINTYRE, ARCHITECT

THE FENCE AND GATE-
POSTS OF THE PEIRCE-
NICHOLS HOUSE ARE
BUILT FROM THE MCIN-
TYRE DESIGNS, WHILE
THE HANDSOME URNS
WERE CARVED FROM
SOLID BLOCKS OF
WOOD BY THE MASTER-
CARVER HIMSELF.

FACADE OF THE PEIRCE-NICHOLS HOUSE; *(below)* THE STABLE AND CARRIAGE HOUSE

BROAD STREET

CHESTNUT STREET, THE FIRST ARCHITECTURAL STREET IN AMERICA, IN SUMMER AND WINTER

To many minds Salem's crowning glory will always be Chestnut Street. This magnificent broad thoroughfare, laid out in 1796, preserves intact the atmosphere of the prosperous days of clipper ships and merchant princes, when Salem shipping was supreme. Today its trees have grown until they arch the roadway and its brick sidewalks are worn thin, but its imposing three-story mansions are still immaculately groomed. Its doorways and fences, without a peer in America, sparkle freshly-painted in the sunlight.

No. 26 HOFFMAN-SIMPSON HOUSE (*c.* 1827)   No. 19   PEABODY-RANTOUL HOUSE (1810)

Chestnut Street Doorways

No. 10   LITTLE HOUSE (1804)   No. 29   DODGE-SHREVE HOUSE (1817)

6

SPRINGTIME SUNSET ON CHESTNUT STREET

CHESTNUT STREET DETAILS—IRONWORK ON THE ELLIPTICAL PORCH OF THE
BARSTOW-WEST HOUSE (1804); *(below)* THE FACADE OF THE PHILLIPS HOUSE

SPRING MORNING ON CHESTNUT STREET

WHERE CHESTNUT STREET BUYS ITS PROVISIONS

MIDWINTER IN CHESTNUT STREET BACK YARDS AND *(opposite)* AT THE PICKERING HOUSE

BALDWIN-LYMAN HOUSE
WASHINGTON SQUARE

PHILLIPS HOUSE
CHESTNUT STREET

LORING-EMMERTON HOUSE
ESSEX STREET

Salem Gate-posts

It is perfectly safe to make the statement that Salem's gate-posts and fences are the finest in the country. These three examples give an idea of their sensitive detail, but it would take many more pages to illustrate the remarkable diversity of their designs.

Afternoon shadows make fascinating patterns out of Chestnut Street porches. This is No. 39 *(opposite)*.

HAMILTON HALL, SINCE 1805 THE SCENE OF SALEM FESTIVITIES

HAMILTON HALL (1805)—SAMUEL McINTYRE, ARCHITECT

Named in honor of Alexander Hamilton, who visited Salem in 1800 and had
many fervent admirers there, Hamilton Hall retains most of its McIntyre features,
including the Palladian windows and his famous carved eagle. The ballroom is
a masterpiece of sedate simplicity. Here Lafayette dined with 300 guests at the
time of his memorable visit in 1824. It has been the center of social life in Salem
for many generations, a symbol of the dignity, the decorum which is the essence
of Chestnut Street.